EDGE BOOKS

BEHIND THE SCENES WITH THE PROS

BEHIND THE SCENES OF PRO BASKETBALL

BY CATHERINE ANN VELASCO

CAPSTONE PRESS
a capstone imprint

Edge Books are published by Capstone Press,
1710 Roe Crest Drive, North Mankato, Minnesota 56003
www.capstonepub.com

Library of Congress Cataloging-in-Publication Data
Names: Velasco, Catherine Ann, author.
Title: Behind the scenes of pro basketball / by Catherine Ann Velasco.
Description: North Mankato, Minnesota : Capstone Press, [2019] | Series: Behind the scenes with the pros | Includes bibliographical references and index. | Audience: Age 8-14. | Audience: Grade 7 to 8.
Identifiers: LCCN 2018043408 (print) | LCCN 2018054964 (ebook) |
ISBN 9781543554298 (ebook) | ISBN 9781543554243 (hardcover) | ISBN 9781543559187 (pbk.)
Subjects: LCSH: Basketball--United States--Training--Juvenile literature. | Basketball players--United States--Health and hygiene--Juvenile literature. | Basketball players--United States--Conduct of life--Juvenile literature. | Basketball players--United States--Charitable contributions--Juvenile literature. | Basketball players--United States--Salaries, etc.--Juvenile literature. | National Basketball Association.
Classification: LCC GV885.1 (ebook) | LCC GV885.1 .V45 2019 (print) | DDC 796.323/64--dc23
LC record available at https://lccn.loc.gov/2018043408

Editorial Credits
Bradley Cole, editor; Craig Hinton, designer; Ryan Gale, production specialist

Photo Credits
AP Images: Rick Bowmer, cover, 5, Alex Brandon, 17; Icon Sportswire: Bahram Mark Sobhani/San Antonio Express-News/ZUMA Press, 27, Daniel Gluskoter, 19, Michele Sandberg, 29, Torrey Purvey, 20, Zumapress, 25; Newscom: Albert Gea/Reuters, 11, Brian Kersey/UPI, 15, JF Moliere/Maxi Basket/SIPA, 23, John Rivera/Icon SMI 426, 7; Rex Features: Rolex Dela Pena/Epa, 9; Shutterstock Images: Sebastian Studio, 13

Design Elements
Shutterstock Images: Graphic Dealer

Printed in the United States 5510

TABLE OF

CONTENTS

TRAINING LIKE A PRO

LeBron James carries a tractor tire down a street in Miami, Florida. It's the off-season and most players are taking a break from basketball. James is already getting ready for the next season. He is known as one of the best players in the National Basketball Association (NBA). James knows what he has to do behind the scenes to be successful.

James often says playing basketball in the NBA is a year-round job. When he doesn't have a game, James is focused on helping his body prepare for the next one. He trains hard all year to survive an 82-game season and long playoff runs. He understands that basketball is more than a game played in front of fans. It is a career with many parts that fans don't see. Take a behind-the-scenes peek at life in the NBA.

NBA players train hard all year to be the strongest and best they can be.

LONG GRIND TO THE NBA

For 10 years Andre Ingram played basketball in the NBA's **developmental league**. This league is called the G League. In 2018 his NBA dream finally came true. At age 32 Ingram got a call from the Los Angeles Lakers. The team wanted to add him to their roster for the final two games of the season.

Ingram dazzled basketball fans during his first NBA game. He scored 19 points and fired up the crowd with four 3-pointers. Fans chanted "MVP!" when he was at the free-throw line. They knew he had waited a long time for this moment.

developmental league—a league that helps players get better

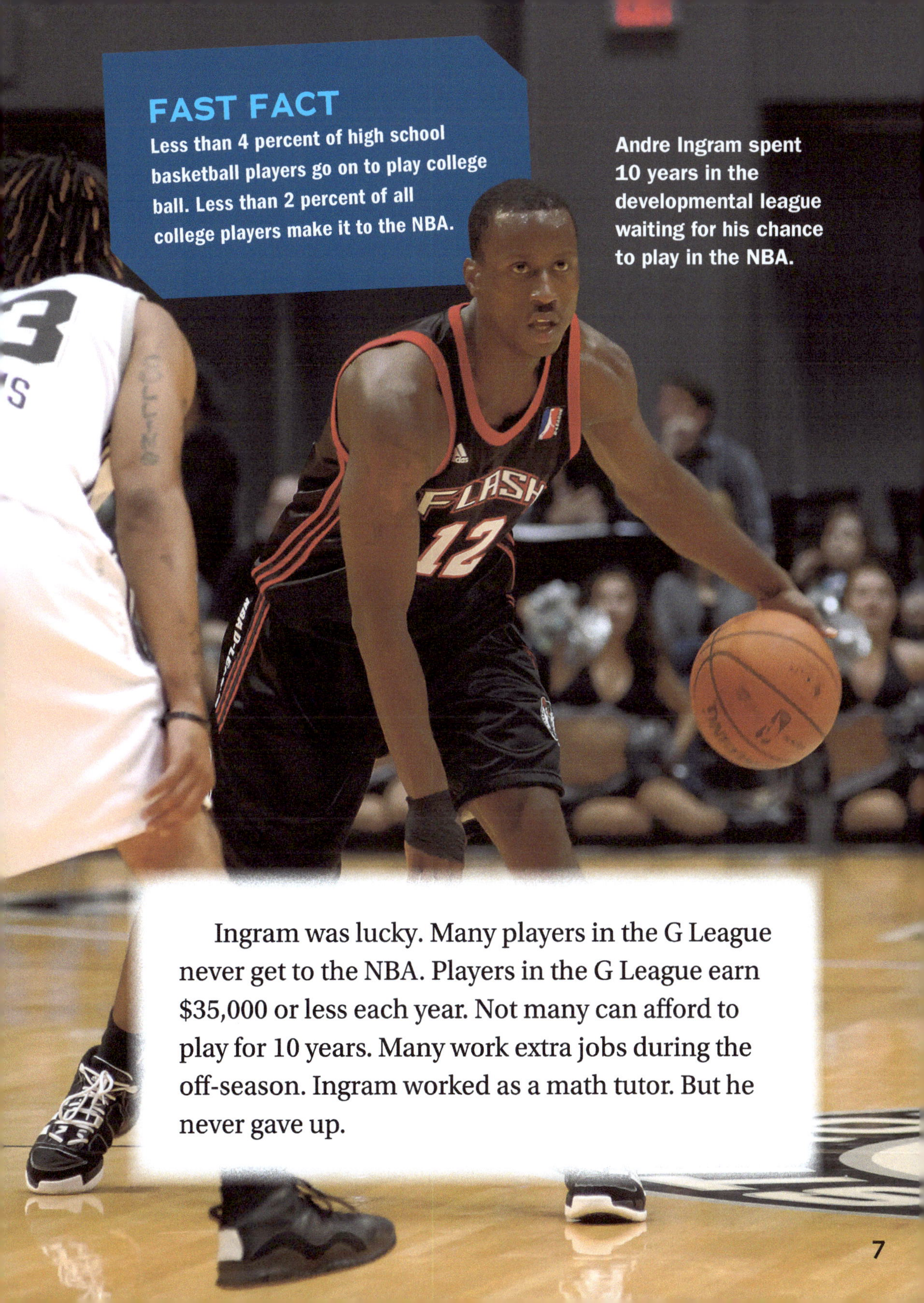

FAST FACT

Less than 4 percent of high school basketball players go on to play college ball. Less than 2 percent of all college players make it to the NBA.

Andre Ingram spent 10 years in the developmental league waiting for his chance to play in the NBA.

Ingram was lucky. Many players in the G League never get to the NBA. Players in the G League earn $35,000 or less each year. Not many can afford to play for 10 years. Many work extra jobs during the off-season. Ingram worked as a math tutor. But he never gave up.

GAME PREPARATION

The NBA season is a busy time for players. The regular season includes 82 games and lasts nearly six months. Players rarely get more than two days between games. Many games are played on back-to-back nights. This doesn't leave a lot of time for players to recover from previous games.

Teams try to help players get the most out of practices. The Sacramento Kings have tried doing fewer physical practices. They replaced some of their regular workouts with mental practices. At these practices, players watch videos of previous games and try to see what they can do better.

FAST FACT

Players prepare mentally before games in different ways. Some players listen to exciting music while others might sit quietly to clear their heads.

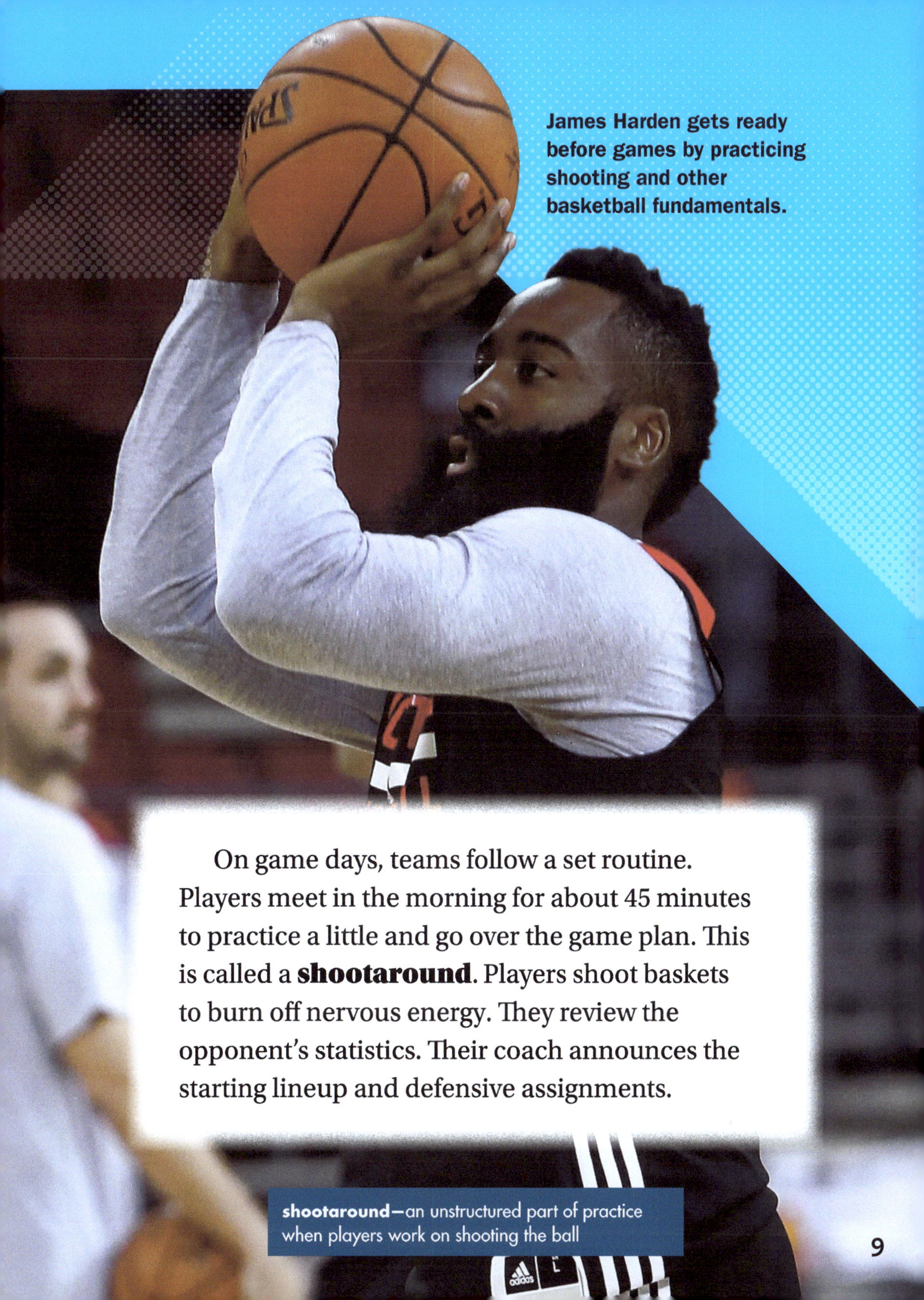

James Harden gets ready before games by practicing shooting and other basketball fundamentals.

On game days, teams follow a set routine. Players meet in the morning for about 45 minutes to practice a little and go over the game plan. This is called a **shootaround**. Players shoot baskets to burn off nervous energy. They review the opponent's statistics. Their coach announces the starting lineup and defensive assignments.

shootaround—an unstructured part of practice when players work on shooting the ball

Recovery AFTER GAMES

Postgame recovery is incredibly important during the long season. Basketball players need to heal quickly from sore muscles and bruises. Some do unusual things to take care of their bodies.

LeBron James of the Los Angeles Lakers wears full-body tights immediately after a game. The special tight-fitting compression clothing increases blood flow and reduces swelling. It speeds up the recovery process. He also plunges into an ice bath to reduce swelling.

FAST FACT

LeBron James spends approximately $1.5 million per year to keep his body in tip-top shape. His personal team includes a recovery coach, trainers, personal chefs, and masseuses.

Other players, such as Chicago Bulls guard Zach LaVine, use cupping therapy. A therapist places special cups on the player's skin for a few minutes to create suction. This helps reduce pain and soreness, improve blood flow, and speed up muscle recovery.

Many players get massages after games to help recover. Some players get traditional massages. Others have found new styles of massage therapy. For example, therapists might use special handheld tools that jab the muscles very quickly. The tools help loosen up tight muscles.

Players ice joints after games to help reduce swelling and soreness.

EAT AND SLEEP

What NBA players eat and how much they sleep is very important. Food gives them energy for training and playing hard in games. They avoid eating a heavy meal before a game so they won't feel sluggish on the court. They refuel after the game. Sleep helps players recover too.

After a game, LeBron James eats a meal packed with **protein** and **carbohydrates**, such as chicken and pasta. This helps him repair his muscles and restore his energy reserves.

Players make sure to get enough sleep. They often take naps. Sleep experts talk to teams about ways to get more and better sleep. Players who get nine hours of sleep react more quickly than those who get less sleep.

protein—a substance found in all living plant and animal cells; foods such as meat, cheese, eggs, beans, and fish are sources of dietary protein
carbohydrate—a substance found in foods such as bread, rice, cereal, and potatoes that gives you energy

JARED DUDLEY'S MEAL PLAN

Jared Dudley is a veteran forward. His meal plan includes a great deal of high-energy, nutritious foods.

Breakfast: eggs, fruit, or oatmeal. The oatmeal helps keep him full.

Lunch: chicken, tuna, or turkey sandwich. The carbohydrates in the bread help him restore his energy. The meat provides the protein he needs to rebuild his muscles.

Snack: trail mix or a salad with salmon or baked chicken. If he wants sweets, he'll have a small frozen fruit treat or a sweetened yogurt. Eating healthy snacks helps keep him from overeating at meals.

Dinner: chicken with lettuce, spinach, asparagus, or another vegetable. If his team wins a game on the road, he has dessert. But it's just one chocolate chip cookie.

A mix of carbohydrates and protein keeps players full and helps repair their muscles.

REHAB

Players train hard to stay strong, which helps them prevent injuries. But injuries still happen. Ankle and knee injuries are common in the NBA. Players can sprain an ankle when they land after jumping. Knee injuries can happen when someone pivots or changes direction quickly. Injuries can sideline a player for an entire season or even end a career. From the minor to the serious, all injuries need **rehabilitation**, or rehab.

Many people thought Paul George's career was over when he suffered a bad fracture in his right leg during a **scrimmage** in 2014. George worked hard in rehab. Lifting weights helped strengthen his leg. Stretching helped him with flexibility. Coordination exercises helped George with **muscle memory**.

rehabilitation—therapy that helps an athlete recover from an injury
scrimmage—a practice game
muscle memory—the ability to automatically repeat a familiar movement through practice and repetition

Injuries and rehab have kept Derrick Rose out of multiple games.

George started playing in games again eight months later. The next season, he played better than ever.

FROM INJURY-PRONE TO MVP

Before 2013 Golden State's Stephen Curry sprained his ankle many times and had to have two surgeries. He repeatedly stressed his ankles too much when he changed direction. To help prevent more ankle injuries, his trainer developed a workout to strengthen Curry's core and lower body. With more strength in his hips and core, Curry put less strain on his ankles. As part of the workout, Curry lifted a barbell from a standing position. This move is called a dead lift. He started lifting 200 pounds (91 kilograms). A year later, he was lifting 400 pounds (181 kg). The plan worked. Curry returned to basketball and even won the NBA's Most Valuable Player (MVP) award in 2015 and 2016.

core—the muscles around the trunk of the body

OFF-SEASON TRAINING

When a player's season comes to an end, the work isn't over. Players keep training even during the off-season. Players might spend hours on a court practicing different parts of the game, such as shooting, rebounding, defense, and ball-handling. They often work on building strength with weight training. All the off-season work is done so players can perform even better the next season.

Boston Celtics guard Kyrie Irving has worked with a ball-handling specialist to improve the mechanics of his game. Irving dodged basketballs while dribbling a ball through figure-eight drills. He performed other drills that focused on catching a basketball and dribbling.

Stephen Curry works on his dribbling with specific drills.

The off-season is also a good time for players to learn new moves or shots. Players sometimes look at what another player is doing and try to imitate it. Dirk Nowitzki became famous for his ability to make a fadeaway jumper. The shot is taken while in the air and jumping away from the defender to create space. Nowitzki starts his shot by leaning back on one foot. Kevin Durant saw Nowitzki's shot and started working on it during the off-season. It eventually became a valuable weapon for Durant.

TRADES AND FREE AGENTS

Each summer some players are traded before the season starts. Other times players start the season on one team and finish it on another. But the trade must be final before the trade deadline in February each season. The NBA must approve all trades for them to be official.

A team's front-office staff handles trades. The general manager makes the final trade decision. But he receives advice from other team employees, including assistant general managers, the president of basketball operations, and scouts.

Teams can trade a player for another player, money, or even **draft picks**. Trading the player might make the team better or save the team money. Teams sometimes trade their best players for draft picks to try to improve in the future.

draft pick—a team's opportunity to select a new player during the organized process of adding new players

General Manager Bob Myers (right) helped announce the signing of free agent Kevin Durant with the Golden State Warriors.

As the front office makes trade decisions, it must keep the team's salary cap in mind. The cap limits how much money a team can spend on its players. Teams are fined for going over the salary cap.

Enes Kanter (right) and Russell Westbrook became good friends when they were teammates.

FAST FACT

A player might have his agent include a player option in his contract. This agreement gives the player the option to stay or leave the team when his contract expires.

A player can also change teams as a free agent. A player is considered a free agent when his contract runs out. He is then able to sign with any team. His agent contacts interested teams and **negotiates** a deal for the player with his new team.

Players make friends with teammates during their careers. As players move to different teams, former teammates often stay friends. Enes Kanter played with Russell Westbrook in Oklahoma City. Kanter was traded to the New York Knicks but still keeps in touch with Westbrook.

As new contracts are negotiated, players, agents, and teams aren't the only ones involved. The National Basketball Players Association is the NBA players' union. Its mission is to ensure that the rights of NBA players are protected. The union negotiates with the league and team owners over things that affect all players. The union negotiates minimum and maximum salaries. It also looks at the number of practices during the off-season and the maximum length of free-agent contracts.

negotiate—to bargain or discuss something to come to an agreement

Endorsements

NBA players can make a lot of money from **endorsements** and commercials for products. The NBA's 10 biggest endorsement stars earned a total of $234 million off the court in 2018. That is more endorsement money than the top 10 U.S. football players, baseball players, and hockey players combined.

Players endorse shoes, sports drinks, athletic clothing, and products and services beyond basketball, such as car insurance and cell phones. Agents help players negotiate the best deals. Many players see these endorsements as a good way to get more attention as players and as celebrities.

endorsement—a statement or advertisement in support of a product or service

The star with the most endorsements is LeBron James. His endorsements include Nike, Sprite, Beats by Dre, Kia Motors, Intel, and Blaze Pizza. He sells more of his signature shoes for Nike each year than any other active athlete.

FAST FACT

LeBron James has a lifetime contract with Nike. No other NBA player has a lifetime endorsement deal. James's contract with Nike is worth more than $1 billion.

Companies pay basketball players such as LeBron James to advertise products.

HANDLING THE MEDIA

The media covers all NBA games. It's important for players to handle the media well to create a good public image. Reporters can interview players before and after games. After games, players might be interviewed on the court, in the locker room, or in a press conference. Players also may have to talk to media members after practice. For some players, having the media around can be overwhelming. But players still need to stay positive, open, and patient with the reporters. Some players handle this pressure better than others.

FAST FACT

Many players create "burner" accounts on social media platforms. That allows them to follow what is being said about them. They can even join conversations without anyone knowing they are behind the accounts.

Like other NBA stars, Chris Paul (center) meets with the media for interviews after games and practices.

Media members sometimes interview players away from the basketball scene for feature stories. Players can open up about their life off the court. They can also connect with their fans by writing their own articles for *The Players' Tribune*. This media company shares athletes' stories.

The media and fans pay close attention to players' social media accounts. Players have to be careful about what they post on social media. They can make headlines if they post something inappropriate. Stephen Curry says he reads every post again before he sends it. If he sees something that makes him hesitate, he doesn't post it. Some players' agents help manage their public relations after social media mishaps.

COACHING STYLES

Every coach has his or her own style. Some coaches are good teachers and help develop players. Others are good at motivating their players to compete and win.

Gregg Popovich has been an NBA coach for more than 20 years. He has found success by forming close relationships with his players. Players want to play for the Spurs because Popovich gets to know his players really well. He sometimes shares meals with his players. He teaches players to be unselfish both on and off the court. Following his example, former San Antonio Spurs center Tim Duncan negotiated a contract for less money in order to help his team.

Phil Jackson also succeeded using this strategy. He coached all-time greats such as Michael Jordan, Scottie Pippen, Kobe Bryant, and Shaquille O'Neal. Because Jackson got to know his players, he understood their needs. He coached each player differently based on what he learned about them. For example, Jackson gave Bryant more freedom on offense. This is how Jackson got the entire team to play well together.

FAST FACT

Jackson gave personalized book recommendations to each player. He often picked books to help players develop leadership skills. Sometimes he recommended a book just because he thought the player would enjoy reading it.

Gregg Popovich of the San Antonio Spurs manages his team by having close relationships with his players.

CHARITY WORK

Many pro basketball players want to strengthen their communities and help people in need. Players support causes close to their hearts. Some players start their own foundations or charities.

LeBron James set up the LeBron James Family Foundation in 2006. It provides students in James's hometown of Akron, Ohio, with full **scholarships** to the University of Akron. The **mentorship** program starts in third grade and follows students throughout middle school and high school. More than 1,100 students have been mentored by the program. He also announced the opening of I Promise School in 2018. The school is for at-risk third and fourth graders. James and the Akron public school system helped plan the school.

scholarship—a grant or prize that pays for a student to go to college or follow a course of study
mentorship—the advice or guidance given by a mentor

Kevin Durant helped citizens of Oklahoma when he played for the Oklahoma City Thunder. A tornado struck the Oklahoma City area in 2013. Durant donated $1 million to help citizens rebuild after the tornado. The Thunder and the NBA also donated $1 million to the cause.

Dwyane Wade reads to kids at a holiday charity event in Miami, Florida.

GLOSSARY

carbohydrate (kar-boh-HYE-drate)—a substance found in foods such as bread, rice, cereal, and potatoes that gives you energy

core (KOR)—the muscles around the trunk of the body

developmental league (di-vel-uhp-MEN-tuhl LEEG)—a league that helps players get better

draft pick (DRAFT PIK)—a team's opportunity to select a new player during the organized process of adding new players

endorsement (in-DORS-muhnt)—a statement or advertisement in support of a product or service

mentorship (MEN-tor-ship)—the advice or guidance given by a mentor

muscle memory (MUHSS-uhl MEM-uh-ree)—the ability to automatically repeat a familiar movement through practice and repetition

negotiate (ni-GOH-shee-ate)—to bargain or discuss something to come to an agreement

protein (PROH-teen)—a substance found in all living plant and animal cells; foods such as meat, cheese, eggs, beans, and fish are sources of dietary protein

rehabilitation (re-huh-bi-li-TAY-shun)—therapy that helps an athlete recover from an injury

scholarship (SKAHL-ur-ship)—a grant or prize that pays for a student to go to college or follow a course of study

scrimmage (SKRIM-ij)—a practice game

shootaround (SHOOT-uh-round)—an unstructured part of practice when players work on shooting the ball

READ MORE

Bradley, Michael. *Stathead Basketball: How Data Changed the Sport.* Stathead Sports. North Mankato, Minn.: Compass Point Books, 2019.

Frederick, Shane. *Basketball's Record Breakers.* Record Breakers. North Mankato, Minn.: Capstone, 2017.

Kramer, S. A. *Basketball's Greatest Players.* Step Into Reading. New York: Random House, 2015.

INTERNET SITES

Use FactHound to find Internet sites related to this book.

Visit www.facthound.com

Just type in 9781543554243 and go.

INDEX